My Journey as a Highly Sensitive Person with Anxiety

How I went from an Emotional Mess to Confident Woman and You Can Too

By: Lauren R. Stewart

www.findyourmagichsp.com

Chapters:

1 – My story

2 – Learning to manage your emotions & removing bad energy

3 – Dealing with Overthinking, Worry, Stress, and Anxiety

4 – Trusting Yourself and the Universe

5 – Manifesting your dreams

6 – Dealing with the world aka sometimes a scary place

7 – Developing confidence and self-love

8 – Finding your HSP Magic

My Story

If you're reading this, you are likely a highly sensitive person and/or have experienced anxiety. Perhaps you are reading this to understand someone in your life. Either way, kudos to you! I hope to tell a little bit more about how I grew up, some challenges I experienced and some great opportunities and experiences that happened because I took the steps to learn to love myself and think more positively. I hope that in reading this that you start to learn to love yourself, love your highly sensitive soul, learn to deal with anxiety a little better and find your magic (more on that later...). Here's my story...

Let me first start by saying I had a great childhood. I was an only child, but it didn't bother me. I liked to spend time with adults and I made plenty of friends at school. In fact, even though I was a shy introvert, my mom likes to remind me how I would come home from school all the time saying, "Mom, I made a new friend today!" with a big smile on my face. I got good grades, except sometimes math (thanks to my creative writer brain that didn't really get all of those calculations). However, school and other social engagements were often a scary place. My happy place was at home with a book, drawing, writing or playing on the computer. I liked being alone. I was that kid at school crying and calling my mom all the time to pick me up. I was also that kid who was so nervous to go to other kid's birthday parties that I would freak out and not want to go. However, once I was there and settled in, I usually had a great time. Now I realize, I was just a highly sensitive kid who was also an introvert (school and parties often cater to extroverts) and I had no clue how to manage my emotions or deal with all of the external happenings at school or at parties. I think my parents hoped I would grow out of it and my teachers ranged from being supportive and kind to a little cruel about the whole thing. At the time, I don't think there was much research being done about highly sensitive people or introverts and it certainly wasn't something readily available for teachers or parents, so I don't blame them at all for any of their reactions.

As I reached middle school, it was an up and down rollercoaster. I am sure throwing hormones into the mix didn't help. I remember getting dial-up Internet for the first time and slowly researching my symptoms when I told people that "I felt weird" and was experiencing all of these strange physical and emotional symptoms. Every page seemed to result in one thing: anxiety. Things were finally starting to make sense a little bit. However, even up to recently, I tended to use my anxiety as a crutch. 'I can't do that' because I have anxiety. I don't even want to tell you how many plans I've ditched in my life because I was feeling too anxious or nervous to go. You might be able to relate. That is no way to live your life. I've learned that no matter what cards you're dealt in life, it is up to you on how you deal with them. You can sit and wallow and think that no one understands you or you can take those little steps to learn to understand yourself more. You can take bigger steps, like reading this book and actively working on yourself, to help you work through any issues that come up in your life. However, there are times when you do need to "ditch" plans to rest your body or your mind. But if you find yourself sitting at home alone, afraid to do anything, that is when you need to get yourself some help from a professional.

I went on to high school and college and experienced a lot of normal ups and downs of navigating your teens and twenties. In this book, I will share more of my experiences and stories in hopes that they can give you a little bit of hope if you are experiencing something similar or need a real-life experience to compare to.

With sharing a little bit of my past and my story, I hope that it helps you to not feel so alone. I hope that you realize how many people out there are also highly sensitive like you or have anxiety like you. You've never alone and there is always support out there for you.

In this book, I also want to ask you questions in each chapter to help you learn more about yourself. Think of it as a workbook of sorts. I want to teach you everything I've learned over the years through research, trial and error and my own past experiences to help you learn to manage your emotions and live a happier life. Even if you picked up this book and you aren't highly sensitive or you don't have anxiety, I think you can still take away something. Please remember that I am not a licensed therapist and this book is not considered medical advice. It is just based on the knowledge that I have learned through research and experience. I also highly recommend that you get a new journal to go with this book. Treat yourself to that fancy journal you've been eyeing for a while. You'll need it to write down what you've learned about yourself, what you want to accomplish and any other thoughts and feelings that arise as you go through this book. Now let's get started.

Learning to manage your emotions and removing bad energy

First of all, when I say to "manage your emotions", I don't mean to make them more comfortable or change for other people. I simply mean to learn to deal with life as best as you can, being true to yourself and having healthy emotions. As a highly sensitive person, this can be one of the most difficult things to deal with. For many people, even when they are upset, they can keep their feelings in and stay calm until they have the time and space to properly vent and deal with the emotions. I know many other HSPs have asked me for advice on how to manage their emotions so they aren't a blubbering mess 24/7. Most HSPs (I say most because everything is different and unique!) feel each emotion more strongly than non-HSPs, might cry more often and might take things more personally than they should because they feel other's energies. First and foremost, you need to learn how to love and accept yourself just the way you are and be cool with the fact that you might cry more than the average person. Once you accept this, it can be easier to deal when unpleasant or embarrassing emotions arise. Then you aren't giving yourself the added stress of beating yourself up for having these oftentimes uncontrollable emotions in the first place. I remember growing up, I started to hate going to the movies with my friends. Unless it was a full-on comedy, most movies have tear-jerker parts and I always cry at random scenes in movies. I would get embarrassed by the fact that I teared up and the rest of my friends didn't. As I got older, I realized that crying at sad parts of movies is completely normal, especially for highly sensitive people. And guess what? My friends rarely ever noticed that I was crying anyway. In fact, I recently went on a trip with my boyfriend and unknowingly picked a sad movie to watch on the plane. I was balling my eyes out and he didn't even notice because he was so sucked into the movie he was watching. I'm sure no one else on the plane noticed either.

Remember, it may help or hurt, depending on the situation, but the truth is people don't notice you as much as you think. You are always more critical of yourself. In fact, sometimes the thing you dislike about yourself is something that others love about you! My boyfriend doesn't see my sensitivity as a burden. He loves how caring and empathetic I am.

Second, make sure you are always taking care of your basic needs. Being hungry, thirsty, over-tired or having some other health issue can make you feel like you are riding a rollercoaster of unpleasant emotions. I know I always get overemotional when I am not feeling well. Often when you are busy and life gets overwhelming, your basic needs are the first to get forgotten about. Make sure you eat regularly, eat healthy meals, drink lots of water, get plenty of sleep and do things that relax you. Ever heard the quote, "I'm sorry for what I said when I was hungry"? When you aren't feeling well, you're hungry, dehydrated, tired or even PMSing for us girls out there, you can't regulate your emotions and work through things as effectively as when you are feeling your best. So, remember to take care of yourself first. Pack your fridge or your everyday bag with healthy snacks and a bottle of water. Experiment with different morning and night routines to get your best sleep and start your day fresh. Your body knows what works best for you, so start to listen better.

Now that we covered basic needs, let's work on some ways to manage your emotions and get rid of any bad energy that you may have picked up from negative thoughts or picked up from others around you.

Journaling is one of my favorite ways to deal with my emotions. If I don't feel like writing things out, I will also simply talk things out with myself. I might sound like a loony tune, but I only do this when I'm home alone or driving alone (my dogs don't judge me, sometimes they even listen! hehe). Sometimes just venting out loud or writing it out can be enough to let things go or realize the true core of the issue. If you're feeling overwhelmed by the number of things you have to do, write them out as well. If you are simply worrying about everything under the sun, give yourself five minutes to write out a "worry list". Write down everything you're worried about and everything you're stressing about and then rip it up! Let it go. Take a deep breath.

If you have a hard time dealing with emotions when it regards others, take the time to really think if this person is needed in your life. Sometimes we can't avoid toxic people in our lives. They might show up at work or in our families, but there are steps you can take to stop giving them so much control over how you feel. Remember that people can say and do anything to you, but it is always up to you in how you react. Easier said than done, right?

Make sure to set some boundaries with others. Is your crazy boss calling you at all hours of the day and night? Set boundaries and make sure they know when your reachable hours are and stop accepting calls at 11 pm. If they still continue to ignore your boundaries, it may be time for a new job. I know change is scary for everyone and it might be particularly debilitating for you, but I promise it can be worth it. Does your family constantly criticize you? Stop spending time with them unless absolutely necessary. When you do see them, take a deep breath and kill them with kindness. If you start to get worked up, leave the room and go for a little walk to clear your head. If you find that trying to talk it out and diffuse conflict isn't working, talk to a therapist and even bring the person with you to help effectively discuss your issues in a neutral setting and set real-life boundaries. And by all means, if you have friends that treat you like crap, say goodbye! Sometimes we can't avoid people in our lives that hurt us, but most of the time we can! Toxic people have no place in your life, HSP. Trust your gut and your heart and do what is right for you. If you are constantly coming home tired, feeling negative and uneasy from spending time with a friend, you might want to take a step back.

So, what do you do if you feel like you are picking up bad energy from others? It could be that you have to sit next to a co-worker who is constantly complaining about everything in life and you go home feeling exhausted and negative. One of my favorite ways to get rid of bad energy is to take a shower. As soon as you get home from a place where you feel you've picked up some negative energy or bad vibes, take a nice, warm shower. As you scrub your body, imagine yourself scrubbing away the negative energy as well. It can help put you in a better mindset as you relax for the evening.

Another great way to release negative energy is smudging. If you've never heard of smudging, you take sage or Palo Santo wood and light it on fire for a few minutes (be extremely careful!) and then blow it out. You'll see smoke start to appear. Wave it around your home, your body, even your pets to clear out negative energy and invite in better vibes. I like to say a prayer or positive thought as I do this to invite in even more positivity. You can buy sage or Palo Santo at most stores that sell crystals and other holistic materials.

If you have spent a lot of time with someone who has hurt you or gave you long-term negative vibes, you might need to try a de-cording exercise. Even if you no longer see or talk to this person, you might find yourself still thinking or dreaming about them and they might cause you pain, even years after you no longer talk. If so, try this exercise. Picture them in your mind and picture a cord going from your heart to theirs. Visualize cutting the cord and letting them go. Visualize how you would feel if you were no longer hurt by them and no longer thought or dreamt about them often. If you are still having negative feelings about them, picture them as a little kid. It is harder to be angry at a child. Practice forgiving them for everything they've done to you. Keep visualizing cutting this cord and meditate on these feelings. Don't be alarmed if they suddenly reach out to you or you run into them after you've done this exercise. You might at first think that it didn't work! But sometimes that is how energy works. Perhaps you just want to let them know that you forgave them and let them go and no longer want to communicate. It might also be a great way to see what feelings get stirred up by hearing from them or seeing them. Journal these thoughts and continue working on letting go of these feelings. This exercise can help you get rid of some pent-up anger and emotions towards others that you have been holding on to, often for a very long time. You can also try journaling your feelings as you practice this de-cording exercise or talking it out with someone you trust. Remember that holding on to these negative feelings isn't hurting them. It is only hurting you, so let it go. It may take efforts and time, but once you finally forgive and heal, you'll start to open up your heart to more positive things to come to you.

For many highly sensitive people and introverts, getting enough rest is very key to managing emotions and keeping a high vibe energy. Make sure you get enough sleep and rest and time alone to process your feelings and emotions. Exercise can also be a great way to keep your emotions regulated and process your feelings.

Get out your journal and answer these questions:

How will you start to remove negative energy?

Is there anyone you feel you need to try 'de-cording' from?

What ways will you start to manage your emotions?

Do you notice that you have a hard time managing your emotions when your basic needs are not met? Write down an example.

Other thoughts from this chapter:

Dealing with Overthinking, Worry, Stress, and Anxiety

How often do you overthink, worry, stress or have anxiety? Be honest here. I used to live in a constant cycle of overthinking, worrying, stressing about everything and feeling anxious every single day. Remember, if you have an anxiety disorder, you may need to talk to a doctor or therapist to get the help that you need. Don't ever be afraid to ask for help.

It happens to the best of us and I do believe that there are seasons of our lives that will be filled with worry and stress. It is natural and life can throw some big curveballs at you. But it is up to you on how you deal.

I believe that feeling unsettled had a major effect on the anxiety and panic attacks that I've had over the years. I have moved 6 times in my adult life, over the span of about 8 years. Some of these living situations have been great and others have been very stressful. Now that I have a house of my own and am living with my boyfriend and two dogs, I do feel that settling in has reduced my anxiety a lot overall in addition to other ways I manage it. Perhaps you have a similar story or you have a situation that causes you a lot of anxiety or stress. Once you realize what is causing you the anxiety, stress, worry or overthinking is when you can start to deal with it. Let's journal to see if we can uncover something new about yourself.

Remember to journal the questions I ask in this book to really uncover how you deal with situations and how you can choose to change your reactions.

What types of situations do you often overthink? What do you worry about?

When do you experience the most stress and anxiety?

If one particular person or situation comes to mind, write that down. For a lot of us, jobs, relationships or life happenings can cause a lot of stress. Now is the time to re-evaluate.

If you constantly feel worried, stressed and anxious at work and when you come home, you might want to think about getting a new job.

If you overthink every little thing in terms of your relationship, you might need to talk it out with that person or you might need to move on.

Your life truly is what you make it. Do you really want to have a relationship that isn't with the man or woman of your dreams? Do you want a job that you dread going to every day?

You can give every excuse in the book. Go ahead, write them all out! Then rip them up! It isn't that I don't care that you don't think you can find another job or relationship or whatever. I care about you and that's why I know you can do so much better than whatever is stressing you out! Changing your life is scary and hard and exhausting, but once you change and find new opportunities come to you, I promise you will be happier. We will learn more about trusting the universe and manifesting your dreams later in this book. For now, let's learn more about how to deal with overthinking, worry, stress and anxiety.

Once you've discovered what is really bringing you down (it may take a while to really figure it out, give yourself time), start to make action plans for change. Baby steps here people! I'm not asking you to quit your job before you have another one. Then you'll just be stressing about money! But if you realize that you want a new job and that will help you to stop worrying and stressing out so much, start with little steps to get you there. Work on your resume, apply for jobs, reach out to old contacts in the job arena you desire… you get the drill.

If you realize your issue is that you really just overthinking, worry and stress about everything in your life, no matter how good or bad it is, try some of these tips:

- Every time you worry, overthink or stress about something minuscule, re-direct your thoughts. You control your thoughts, not the other way around… even though you might not always realize this.
- Have a venting buddy that you trust. Share your worries and stress with someone who listens and understands and do the same for them.
- Make a worry-wart box. Put in there anything that can help you re-direct your thoughts. For example, you could include a journal and a pen, a book, a crossword puzzle or game, your favorite candy, some relaxation tea, or anything else that puts you in a good mood or can help change your thoughts quickly.
- Find your favorite positive quotes and put them up all over your home or work.
- Set aside some worry time each day. Allow yourself to only overthink, stress or worry at this designated time and use this time to think of productive solutions.
- Try meditation or exercise the next time you start worrying or overthinking.

- If you deal with panic attacks, try to find the trigger. Is your blood sugar dipping? Are you dehydrated? Are you dealing with something very stressful and not utilizing proper self-care? There may be a trigger and sometimes there may not be one. Try to have a separate self-care toolkit for panic attacks to help yourself and have others help you. Include notes on how you'd like someone to handle the situation with you, in case you feel you can't communicate properly. Remember to breathe and remind yourself over and over that this awful feeling WILL pass. You'll be okay as tough as it seems. If you experience frequent panic attacks that disrupt your life, talk to your doctor.

Worrying and overthinking is really putting some negative energy out there. If you are constantly thinking about the worst-case scenario, what do you think might actually present itself? For example, if you prepare and study well for a test, but then you overthink every question and worry so much about getting a bad grade, you probably will fail just because you didn't trust yourself and your abilities! You'll probably overthink the questions and change your answers to wrong ones.

Or if you are constantly overthinking your relationship, wondering if your boyfriend or girlfriend really likes you, you are putting out some seriously anxious and low self-esteem vibes. This will probably make your man or woman see you as less attractive and can hurt your relationship that was fine in the first place!

Use your journal or even talk it out and record yourself to stop overthinking and worry. Write or say out loud everything you're stressing out about or worrying about.

If you have minor anxiety or would like to work on lessening your anxiety with the help of professionals, here are some things that have really helped me over the years:

- Staying busy and focusing on helping others. When anxiety hits, instead of sitting on the couch and focusing on the anxiety, focus on something that keeps your mind and your hands busy. Helping others is something that really helps me to bust out of an anxiety funk. Try calling a friend, writing a letter, volunteering or asking if someone needs your help with something.
- Acupuncture and massage. These two things have greatly helped my anxiety. Try them out and see if they work for you.
- Essential oils. There are so many different ways to use essential oils and different oils to try.
- Focus on a healthy diet, exercise and ask your doctor or naturopath for supplements that might work for you.
- I also have a heal your anxiety course that gives you everything I've learned that has lessened my anxiety. Check it out here: https://www.findyourmagichsp.com/heal-anxiety-course

If you have serious anxiety, an anxiety disorder or any other type of serious issue that is interfering with your life, please talk to a therapist or medical professional.

Other thoughts and takeaways from this chapter:

Copyright 2018 Lauren R. Stewart, Find Your Magic as a Highly Sensitive Person ©

Trusting Yourself and the Universe

There is something I am constantly reminding my boyfriend and he is probably sick of hearing it by now. I am always telling him to think positive and believe that good things will come to him. It is the basic law of attraction if you're into that kind of thing. But I truly do believe in my life, when I believed that good things would happen, they did. When I started feeling down on myself and felt like nothing good would ever happen ever again, that's when I was in a dark place.

I'm not saying you have to be rainbows and sunshine every day. That isn't realistic. We all have different seasons in our lives. Sometimes everything is going great and we are happy every single day. Other times, things go wrong. We might experience heartbreak, grief, lose our jobs, or simply have a string of bad luck. These things will happen no matter how positive you are because that's life. Wouldn't life be extremely boring if things were just peachy all of the time? However, I do truly believe that when we focus on the positives, our bad times don't last as long and we see that everything happens for a reason. It also helps us to preserve and find strength from bad times instead of letting it ruin us.

As a highly sensitive person, you are definitely more in tune with the energies of the world. It has been said that highly sensitive people are better at manifesting because of this. So, think of how amazing your life can be if you get into that positive energy!

You might be wondering; how do you start trusting yourself and the Universe (or God or insert whatever you like to call the bigger picture) has good things in store for you? Depending on where you are in your self-love and positivity journey, this can be difficult or fairly easy.

Let me tell you another little story about myself. I've never liked school that much and college wasn't really an exception. I graduated with a Bachelor's degree in Journalism in 3 ½ years because I just wanted to get it over with and start working a job that I loved where I would make more money. I have no clue why but I thought it would be extremely easy, even with a hard job market like Journalism. However, I didn't really want to work in the news. Looking back now, the news and its catastrophic behavior is a nightmare for highly sensitive people so it is kind of funny I picked that anyway. My passion really was creative writing and my college didn't offer any degree like that at the time so I just picked the only major that had to do with writing. Right before graduation, I found a job opportunity working public relations for a small company. I thought it would be perfect, especially since I would be working out of her home. What a win for my introvert soul, I thought. However, as I started the job, I realized that our personalities did not click and the job just really wasn't for me. I came home crying almost every day that I worked. I didn't know what to do. I thought I had found a perfect job and now I was forced to go back to square one. I didn't know it at the time, but things were set into motion. It was very stressful to think about being thrown back into a tough job market.

While I only worked that job for about a month, I did meet a friend of my previous boss and we hit it off. She was starting her own health and wellness website and needed a paid intern. I got the gig and it was a much better fit! As I started to work for her, I realized how passionate I was about writing for health and wellness websites. I started to meet her friends and was offered new work opportunities. My freelance business was growing. When I graduated, I had no idea I wanted to freelance or even any idea that I could! At the same time, a previous unpaid internship with a nonprofit organization I had worked for had reached out to me and asked me to come back and work a few paid hours. I decided to just keep taking any opportunity that came my way.

I started to realize my dream of writing and working from home. This wasn't something that my family approved of sometimes. They wanted me to find an office job, work 9-5 so I could get a better paycheck, insurance, 401k and all of that. I knew that working in an office with a set schedule, doing work I wasn't passionate about wouldn't give me my best life and it wouldn't make me happy at all. So, I persisted and I worked hard and tried to ignore the critiques from others. During times that my freelance business was slow, I would pick up side jobs or part-time jobs, especially when I was out living on my own. I had faith that things would work out and I could fulfill my dream of working at home, on my own schedule.

At the time this book is published (about 8 years after graduation from college), I still work for that nonprofit. My hours and my pay rate grew and grew. I also found new freelance opportunities, mostly from referrals from previous clients and some from research and hard work applying. I live in a house that I bought. I have a car that I paid off. All while trying to follow my dreams and working mostly from home. Don't get me wrong, I didn't always have freelance jobs that I was truly passionate about. But what kept me going was my dream of working at home and having a freer schedule that those who work set hours for a company.

It is kind of crazy to see how the wheels were set in motion since I was in college. Had I not seen that advertisement for an internship and applied, I would not have my current job that allowed me to live on my own, buy a house, etc. At the time, I didn't even need any more internship opportunities, I just thought I would add one to look good on my resume. Had I not worked extremely hard at that unpaid internship, they wouldn't have wanted to hire me later. Had I not had that job that wasn't a good fit, I wouldn't have met other people who I went on to work for and loved those jobs.

It helps me so much to look at times of stress and heartache and see the positives that come out of it.

I'll give you another example in relation to love and relationships. I went through a period of time when I was single after a string of failed relationships. I was trying to navigate the world of dating for the first time in my adult life. I was extremely confused and often depressed. I don't think I fully let myself heal or process emotions because I was so focused on finding "the one". I thought finding a new boyfriend was the only thing that would make me truly happy. I remember one year being the darkest of my life. I didn't feel like doing anything and I experienced anxiety and panic attacks almost every single night. Every failed date would send me into a spiral. I was going back to people from the past who weren't right for me just so I wouldn't be alone. I just wanted some attention and comfort. I was looking for love in the wrong places. Eventually, I started to realize my worth and I wasn't going to put up with these guys anymore. I gave myself time away from dating apps and just planned more time with my girlfriends. I started to focus more on myself and I worked harder and was able to move into an apartment by myself for the first time in my favorite city. While I still experienced a lot of anxiety (moving, especially alone for the first time can be tricky!), I was definitely on the mend.

Wouldn't you know at this time when I started to work on myself, that's when I met my current boyfriend? My best friend was getting married and she and her now-husband planned a joint Bachelor/Bachelorette party. I made it clear I was against it and they should do separate parties (I'll admit I was probably obnoxious). Well, wouldn't you know that they didn't listen to me (thankfully!) and that's where I met my current boyfriend! He gives me the kind of love I could have only dreamed of and I feel extremely blessed and excited to see where the future takes us.

The Universe is so funny! As I was writing this chapter, I took a break and it showed up on my phone that I had posted a quote on Facebook 5 years ago... "Sometimes fate is on your side. Other times well, you've kind of sealed your own fate. Either way, you have to trust that whatever's supposed to happen will happen. Besides, somehow you always seem to end up with the person you're meant to be with."

All of these stories aren't meant to make you feel jealous or like my life is now perfect (no one's life is perfect and mine certainly isn't), but to show you clear examples of how you can trust yourself and the Universe to bring you where you want to go. It is meant to show you to trust even in bad times that something good is coming.

Let's work on some examples from YOUR life. Let's get out that journal again!

Think of a clear example of a path where something perceived negative turned into something amazingly positive.

What is something you are working toward in your life?

How can you start to trust yourself and the Universe every day?

Feel free to journal these questions to really dive deep and think about your answers.

Something you can start doing is to trust the opportunities that come to you naturally. Trust and expect that the best opportunities will come to you. After a while, I began to believe that the best is yet to come. I rarely worry about money or work because I truly believe that opportunities will just fall into my lap. This isn't narcissistic, it is simply using the law of attraction. I'm not saying if you are looking for a job that you should just stop applying for jobs. I'm saying that while you actively look for a job and accept new connections, you should trust that the right things will come your way. I love the quote that states, "Whatever is meant for you will never pass you by". If you truly trust and believe that good things will come to you, they will. You might run into an old friend at the grocery store who knows of a great company that is hiring. You might connect with someone you used to work with on Tinder and hit it off this time. You never know. Be open to the amazing possibilities that can happen in your life.

I know that many highly sensitive people, including myself, overthink things a lot. It can be really hard to let go and let the Universe do its thing. You might start to overthink everything! A really good tip to deal with overthinking is to simply write it out or talk it out with someone you trust. Write down or say out loud every single scenario you are overthinking. Sometimes when you actually write down or verbalize a thought, it sounds so silly! When you were thinking and thinking about it, it was terrifying, but when you told someone or wrote it down, you realize you shouldn't even be worrying about it. Of course, just like everything in this book, if you find yourself struggling and nothing is helping, please see a trained professional to help you.

When you start to trust yourself, you'll discover what you really want and need in life. When you start to trust the Universe, the right connections and opportunities will fall into your lap. It is all about staying positive and open.

Other thoughts and takeaways from this chapter:

Copyright 2018 Lauren R. Stewart, Find Your Magic as a Highly Sensitive Person ©

Manifesting Your Dreams

While we are in that state of mind of trusting yourself and the Universe, you might also be interested in learning how to manifest your dreams. So, what does manifesting even mean? To me, manifesting means that you have a clear goal, send it out into the Universe and then be patient and trust that it will happen that way it is supposed to.

For example, say you really want a new relationship. You've been working on yourself and you are so ready for "the one" to come into your life. You might start to write down all of the qualities you wish for in a new partner. You might even write down the time you want them to come into your life. Try to get really specific here and always remain positive. The Universe is more likely to give you what you desire when you remain positive. Instead of saying that you don't want to attract any more jerks, list all of the qualities you would like in a nice man (or woman). Then let it go. Trust that you will get what you desire at the time it is meant to happen. This might not mean that you meet the love of your life tomorrow, but the wheels are being set into motion. If you constantly keep focusing on the negative, that you'll never meet anyone nice or you're sick of waiting, the Universe picks up that energy. But, if you trust that you'll meet someone when the time is right and you just continue on with your daily life, focusing on positive energy, I bet you'll meet someone amazing sooner rather than later.

You can use manifestation for anything you want in life. After I moved into my first apartment by myself, I realized that I actually manifested in a long time ago (before I even really learned about all this stuff!). I used to tell myself all the time that I would live in the downtown area of my favorite city. I used to fantasize about living a cool, single girl life, walking to coffee shops to work and jogging through the park. I didn't obsess about it and I kind of put it out of my mind for a while. Well, low and behold, when I started looking for an apartment of my own, I started looking in that city but I was thinking I wouldn't be able to afford it or find an apartment that was available in a city where lots of people wanted to live. The perfect apartment became available out of the blue. The lady who worked there even told me she was surprised that they had an apartment available at that time. I was able to secure it easily and I went on to live there for a year. I loved it and I would have lived there longer, except I had the opportunity to buy a home and move in with my boyfriend and that was more important to me. But, I remember one day when I realized that I had manifested that apartment all along! In fact, it came up on my phone that I had posted several years earlier that I wanted to live in those exact apartments! I completely forgot that I had posted it. It may have taken a few years, but it needed to happen when I was emotionally and financially ready. So, don't get discouraged if your dreams and goals take time to happen. Things may take a while, but they will be so much more fulfilling when they do if you have to work for it and be patient.

Other times, manifestation might happen right away if you get really good at it! I've seen examples where I come into random money that pays for an unexpected bill. I truly do believe it all depends on your attitude and whether or not you believe that it works.

Let's journal again!

What are you interested in manifesting? Do you want a new job, a new relationship, a new home, a vacation, money, etc.?

Remember to be very specific and stay positive.

Make a vision board to manifest your dreams. A vision board is just a bulletin board or another vessel where you put photos and/or words of your goals and things you want to manifest in your life. You can make one for each area of your life, such as home and work or make one every year. It really is up to you! Once you have your list of things you'd like to manifest, start to search for photos and words that correspond with what you want to manifest. Make a beautiful vision board and hang it in a spot that you'll see every single day. If you need some tips, try searching on Pinterest.

If vision boards aren't your thing, just write down the thing you want to manifest. Remember to be as specific as you can and use positive words. Place it in a spot where you'll see it every day and every time you read it, focus on the fact that it is happening, whether or not you see it in motion yet. Trust and ask for signs that it is coming your way. I love using signs. Signs can help you make decisions or trust that what you desire is on its way to you. When I first learned about using signs, I randomly chose a ladybug and decided that whenever I saw a ladybug (real, cartoon, whatever) that I would remember that I am okay and I am where I am supposed to be. It would help me remember that everything happens for a reason. Ladybugs began popping up everywhere and would instantly calm me whenever I saw one. Signs can help you to make decisions too. You might be wondering if you should quit your job. Suddenly you start seeing stop signs and other similar signals everywhere. This might be your sign to hold off on quitting. Or perhaps you could say if you start seeing dinosaur cartoons, that is a sign to quit. Remember to not make your sign something super obvious that you already see all the time. Make it a little bit weird or difficult, so you know in your heart it is the sign you asked for. For example, if you have a two-year-old that is obsessed with dinosaur cartoons, maybe don't pick that one. :-)

Other thoughts or takeaways from this chapter:

Dealing with the world aka sometimes a scary place

For a highly sensitive person and/or someone with anxiety, the world can sometimes seem like a scary place. Social things that are nerve-wracking for anyone can seem downright impossible. Even something as simple as going out to eat can be scary because you have to worry about crowds, what you are going to order, if the lights are going to be too bright, if the music will be too loud, etc., etc. I remember having a really hard time going out to restaurants and crying because I didn't want to go when I was a kid. I couldn't really articulate why I hated it so much.

Now, I definitely don't love eating out for every meal, but I can definitely enjoy going out to eat at restaurants. I've had my share of panic attacks in a restaurant, which can be extremely embarrassing and debilitating, but it was also a good learning experience.

So, how do you learn to deal with a world that is full of things that may be completely normal and fine to someone else, but is horrible and scary to you?

First of all, remember to treat yourself with kindness. You didn't ask to be born highly sensitive or have anxiety or whatever else you struggle to deal with. Try to focus on the positives of being highly sensitive, like having an extra loving heart, being creative, or whatever else makes you, YOU. You can even try to focus on the positives of having anxiety, like the fact that you know how to make everyone else comfortable because you've dealt with so much.

When you are having a hard time wherever you're at in the world, be kind to yourself and do whatever you need to do at that moment. Sometimes that means leaving and going home. Sometimes it means asking for help. Sometimes it means taking a break to take deep breaths in the bathroom or ordering a glass of water. You get the picture.

To help you deal, here are some things I've learned that help me out in the world that is often catered towards extroverts and non-sensitive people:

Try not to go out anywhere if you are starving or thirsty, even if you're going out to eat. Have a little snack before you go out or always pack a protein bar and a water bottle in your bag. Often anxiety can be caused by your blood sugar being off from being too hungry or thirsty.

Take some essential oils with you. Essential oils are super popular these days and I really believe they work. I like Peppermint oil for any aches, pains or stomach issues. Lavender is great for calming down and relaxing. You can also find many blends for different issues, like anxiety. They also just make you smell really good and who doesn't want that?

Be prepared. I am often the "mom" of the group. You know... that person who always has a snack, water, band-aids, ibuprofen, or whatever you need? That's because I never like to be unprepared in case I start feeling unwell or overwhelmed and it's just a bonus I can usually help others too! It can also help to know the plan. Highly sensitive people and those with anxiety aren't usually known for going with the flow. I used to beat myself up for this and wish I was more adventurous and chill. I still love adventures, but I just like to know what's ahead of me! Ain't nothing wrong with that! Don't be afraid to ask your friends or whomever for the plan ahead so you can mentally prepare yourself. Ask as many questions as you need to feel comfortable.

"If you never ask, the answer is always no." I love that quote because it just shows you should never be afraid to ask for what you need. If you are out with friends and feeling anxious, ask a friend to go outside with you for a minute to breathe. That sometimes is all it takes to feel better. If the loud music is really bothering you somewhere, ask the waitress if they can turn it down at all. They might say no, but at least you tried!

Don't automatically say no to things that make you nervous or scare you. Let me tell you when I was single and going on dates with new guys, I was SO nervous. I would shake, sweat, feel sick and just always want to cancel. In fact, there were times I almost canceled because I was convinced I was sick and not just nervous. Then the guy would cancel and all of a sudden, I would feel perfectly fine. Funny, huh? But, that wouldn't do me any good to stop dating and hide inside all the time, would it? Sometimes things that make you nervous or scare you will turn out to be amazing experiences. If I swore off dating, I would have never met the love of my life. Sure, it took some bad dates to get there, but it was worth it. I now feel confident that I am with the right person because I took the time to have different dating experiences. If you are feeling the nerves before something big or scary, try these tips I've used.

Usually, when I'm nervous, I get hot and sweaty so I would make sure my place was cool and even use an ice pack to "chill out". Make sure to drink plenty of water and have a little snack so you don't pass out or have a blood sugar drop. Try, even if you are feeling sick with nerves. Play your favorite music! I used to throw on some jams and force myself to dance around when I was waiting for a date to pick me up. It would ease the nerves and make me feel a little more confident. Give yourself time to get ready. For me, it would help to take my time to do my makeup and get ready. When you are waiting to do something that scares you, make sure you are doing something. Sitting around will only make you overthink more and get you more nervous. Invite a friend over to help you get ready and talk to you and keep your mind busy while you wait for your date. Pace around if you can't think of anything to do and need to work off some nervous energy. If you find that your anxiety doesn't allow you to live your life, see a therapist or a doctor for help. No shame in that!

The world can be a little harsh at times for HSPs, especially if you have anxiety too. But, remember that being highly sensitive can also allow you to see all of the beauty of the world, more than others can see. Always try to think of the positive.

I'd also like to talk about how to deal with people who think highly sensitive people is a made-up term and they don't understand the way you are. They might even criticize you. This can be extremely difficult for HSPs. There will always be the critics of the world. Now with the Internet, you can be criticized or yelled at by anyone in the world. In fact, when I decided to open up this book for pre-order on Amazon, I started getting negative comments that anyone who tries to help HSPs is a crook, fake, annoying, etc. It hurt me for a second, but I realize that these people are probably just jealous, hurt themselves or crying out for help. Try not to read negative comments and if you come across them, remember that if your heart is in a kind and pure place, you don't have to let others bring you down to their level. Keep doing you. I could have let those comments make me give up this book, but I know that it will help someone out there. Even if it is just one person, putting myself out there to help will always be more important.

Realize that some people just may never understand. It isn't your fault that you can't explain it to them and make them understand. Some people just aren't highly sensitive and based on events in their life, they can't wrap their brain around it. Maybe it will take time. Maybe it won't. Unfortunately, if you have someone like that in your life and they are constantly criticizing you and making you feel bad about yourself, you may need to remove them from your life. Your life is yours and a big part of how you feel can be based on the few people you spend the most time with. So, if your best friend isn't really feeling like a bestie anymore, you may need to step back from spending time with them. This can be a really hard thing for HSPs to do. I know in my past, I have tried to hold on to every single friend I ever made. I would get extremely upset whenever a fight occurred and would blame myself when people treated me like crap. Now I realize that my worth is never dependent on what other's think of me. People can put whatever label they want on me, but it is my choice whether or not I can accept that label or not. Practice this whenever someone tells you to "get over it" or "stop crying" (I know you've heard this about a million times, right? I know I have!).

Have someone read this book or another book or article that explains what being highly sensitive means. Try to explain your experiences and ask for kindness from them. You may need to discuss that you are highly sensitive with a new boss, friend or significant other. This can be scary because no one wants to be criticized for who they are. But just remember that famous quote, "those who mind don't matter and those who matter don't mind." The right significant other, friend, family member or boss will understand or at least attempt to understand. They will treat you with respect and kindness. I know I certainly have family members who think being highly sensitive is completely made up, but they still love and support me. Toxic people in your life might make fun of you and may never understand, no matter how you try to explain it to them. Those people aren't meant to be in your life! There are so many people out there that will love you for who you are and won't ask you to change a thing! Trust me on that one.

Other thoughts and takeaways from this chapter:

Developing Confidence and Self-Love

It can be really difficult to truly develop confidence and self-love these days. Our culture is so dependent on social media and advertisements everywhere. Every product advertiser wants to tell you that if you buy their product you will become smarter, more beautiful, more confident, etc. All you need is to buy this one thing and your life will become perfect. Deep down, we know this isn't true, but all of us get sucked into gimmicky advertising at one time or another. I know I do sometimes, even though I absolutely hate advertising.

When I was little, I was very shy and I didn't have much confidence in myself. I don't think I had much self-love either. I think confidence is something that does grow as you age if you "water" it. If you applaud yourself for your successes and don't beat yourself up too much after failures, you should naturally become more confident in your daily life.

Confidence can be a little tricky. You might become more confident based on what other people say. I know that when I started to date and realized that men found me smart and beautiful, I naturally developed more confidence. But the tricky part with that is what happens when I inevitably met someone who didn't find me smart and beautiful? If I only relied on outside sources for my confidence levels, it would crumble in an instant. But because I worked on feeling confident within myself, I could stay strong. If you work on your self-love, you will naturally be confident too.

So, how do you actually, truly love yourself and feel confident within yourself? Self-love can be a bit trickier. I bet even the most beautiful, smart, seemingly confident person out there has some self-love or image issues.

Be honest: do you truly love yourself? Do you look at yourself in the mirror and see only beauty and no flaws?

Most of us don't, unfortunately. If you are highly sensitive and/or have anxiety, sometimes you can get caught up in negativity, especially about yourself.

Learning self-love can be a whole other book (there are a lot of books on the subject), but I want to just get you started on your self-love journey. You may have already started and just need a refresher.

First of all, write down all of the things you love about yourself.

Next, write down some of the things you might not love or perceive as "flaws".

How can you 'flip these flaws'? For example, I always hated my nose. It has a big bump on it and I have a small red mole on it as well that has never been able to be removed. But, I can learn to love my nose by reminding myself of all the amazing scents I can smell. My nose works as it should and the way it looks shouldn't matter. Even if I do focus on how it looks, my nose looks exactly like my grandpa's. If I hate my nose, I have to hate my grandpa's nose too and well, I just can't do that! What are your examples?

Next, start every day by saying "I love you" to yourself in the mirror. Be thankful for all of the ways your body and mind work for you. When you start to think negatively about anything about yourself, flip it into a positive or make a plan to make it better. Sometimes, I beat myself up for a negative comment I made about someone else. I can't really flip that into a positive, but I can make a commitment right then and there to stop gossiping and be nicer. If you catch yourself beating yourself up for "too big thighs" too often, tell yourself you love your thighs instead. The more positive things you say to yourself, the more likely you are to start believing them.

I also want you to start to "date" yourself. Whether you are single or in a relationship, you need to date yourself too! Dating is how you start to learn about someone else and you tend to have that attraction that makes you see them in an amazing light. Write down a list of things you'd love to do. Pick out a few outfits that make you feel confident. Then make a commitment to date yourself. Go to the movies alone in a fabulous outfit. Treat yourself with the love and respect you want others to do. Give yourself compliments. Do everything you would want and expect an amazing date to do. The more you spend time getting to know yourself and treating yourself with love and respect, the more self-love and confidence will grow.

Other thoughts and takeaways from this chapter:

Copyright 2018 Lauren R. Stewart, Find Your Magic as a Highly Sensitive Person ©

Finding Your HSP Magic

If you've followed my website for a while, you know it is called Find Your Magic as a Highly Sensitive Person. I called it Find Your Magic because I think sometimes it takes a little bit of digging for HSPs to learn to love themselves just the way they are and find out their amazing abilities.

Finding my magic meant that I realized that there wasn't anything wrong with me. Being sensitive wasn't something to "fix". It was something amazing... a true gift. As I've talked about a lot in this book, I truly believe that you can turn any situation into a positive if you work hard enough at it. Being a highly sensitive person is no different. I bet many times in your life you felt so different from others, you wished you were "normal" or like everyone else, you wished you didn't get so overwhelmed and upset, and the list probably goes on and on. But have you ever stopped for a minute and realized your abilities that only come from being highly sensitive?

For example, some amazing qualities of highly sensitive people are creativity, artistic abilities, empathy, amazing listening skills, being a great friend and loved one, anticipating other's needs, kindness, a deep appreciation for the arts, music and other beautiful things in life and just simply being able to live a more meaningful life.

Everyone has special skills they're born with. It might just take a little bit more digging to find yours. Let's do a little journaling to see if we can find out. You might already know your amazing HSP magic qualities and that's great! Let's see if we can uncover some more. Get out your journal again.

Think about a time when you were lit up and just enjoying life to the fullest. What were you doing? Who were you with? How did you feel?

Do you have any hobbies? Do you have anything you might be interested in learning more about? Think about the things you Google when you have downtime or always browse at a store.

What do you think is your true gift in life?

Why do you think you were born highly sensitive?

What are your favorite qualities of being highly sensitive?

What is something good that comes out of having anxiety?

How can you be more positive each day?

I truly hope that this book has helped you. I hope that you are starting to see your worth, how amazing you are, that being highly sensitive is a gift, that having anxiety isn't the end of the world, that you should think positive and believe everything good is happening for you and to learn to love yourself. Come back and go through these chapters whenever you need a little boost. Re-do your journaling questions every few months as you naturally change and things happen in your life. This isn't meant to be a quick read and put away forever.

Remember that you are amazing and your life can be as amazing as you want it to be. You can make anything happen. **You are beautiful. You are strong. You are loved.**

Final thoughts and takeaways from this chapter and this book:

Made in the USA
Lexington, KY
21 July 2019